This Book Belongs To _____

Book Club Edition

Printed in 1991

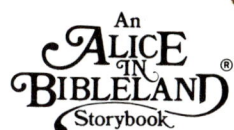

The STORY Of JESUS And HIS DISCIPLES

Written by Alice Joyce Davidson
Designed by Victoria Marshall

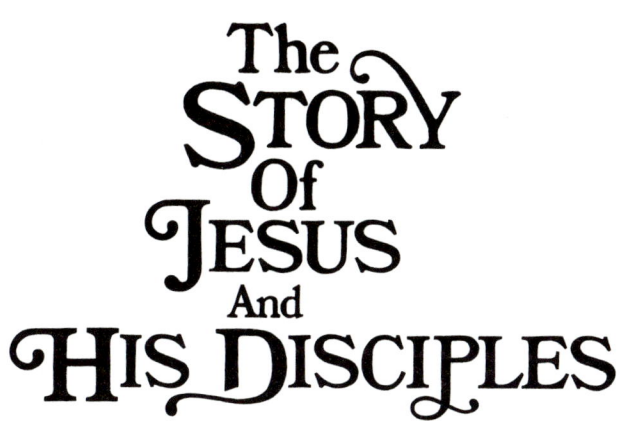

Text copyright © 1989 by Alice Joyce Davidson
Art copyright © 1989 by The C.R. Gibson Company
Published by The C.R. Gibson Company
Norwalk, Connecticut 06856
Printed in the United States of America
All rights reserved

A little girl named Alice
Likes to read her books a lot.
A bench right by her window
Is her favorite reading spot.

Whenever she's not busy
And she has an extra minute,
She reads her Bible storybook
And looks at pictures in it.

One day she read of Jesus,
How He looked until He found
Twelve friends, He called disciples,
To help spread God's Word around.

As Alice read, the airmail bird
Flew to her window sill
And dropped this special message
Which he carried in his bill:

"Reading is the magic key
To take you where you want to be."

Her book became a great big screen,
The screen grew tall and wide,
Then Alice took a little walk
To Bibleland inside.

"The time is right," thought Jesus,
"To go across the land
And tell the people who I meet
God's Kingdom's close at hand.

"I want to teach and preach and help
   Everyone I can,
But I will need disciples
   To carry out this plan."

Andrew was one brother's name.
Peter was the other.
They both seemed good and honest,
And worked well with one another.

James and John were mending nets.
Their boat was on the shore.
Jesus said, "Here's two more men,
The kind I'm looking for.

"Come with Me. You'll never have
To fish for fish again.
Follow Me and you will be
My fishermen of men."

Jesus told His four new friends
The news He wanted spread—
The good news that God's Kingdom
Is coming just ahead.

Jesus was very happy
With the four new friends He found;
But He needed twelve disciples
To help spread the Word around.

So He made friends with Philip,
And with Bartholomew,
And a tax collector, Matthew,
Joined the others, too.

Then came a man whose name was James,
And faithful Simon, too,
Judas joined the others and
All said, "We'll follow You!"

Now Jesus had twelve special friends
And every one of them
Shared His news, and they became
Fishermen of men.

Everywhere they preached God's Word,
Great crowds would follow, too,
And everytime that Jesus spoke,
The crowds just grew and grew.

Jesus spoke in simple language
That all could understand.
And His twelve friends helped spread His news
All across the land.

The time had come for Alice
To leave that Bible scene.
She thought of Jesus and His disciples
As she walked through her screen.

"How good it must have been to be
With Jesus every day,
To be His friend, and spread His word
And follow in His way.

"I'm glad that Jesus is my friend.
He's with me everywhere."
Then Alice put her book away
And knelt and said this prayer:

"Dear Jesus, You're my closest Friend.
You teach me and You guide me.
It feels so good each day to know
That You are here beside me.